THE LIFE OF
JULIUS CAESAR

By
Dr. Nicholas Saunders

School Specialty
Publishing

Columbus, Ohio

THE CAST

Marcus Junius Brutus: *One of Caesar's naval commanders in Gaul. Governor of Transalpine Gaul between 48–46 B.C. A ringleader of Caesar's assassination in 44 B.C.*

Cleopatra: *The daughter of the Egyptian king Ptolemy XII. She became Caesar's lover and had his son Caesarion. Caesar made her queen of Egypt, but her later romance with the Roman general Mark Antony caused arguments with Octavian.*

Mark Antony: *One of Caesar's generals who became quaestor, tribune, then consul in 44 B.C. He joined the Second Triumvirate with Octavian and Lepidus after Caesar's death. Then, he and Cleopatra fought against Octavian in 31 B.C.*

Gaius Julius Caesar Octavianus (Octavian): *Born 63 B.C., Octavian was the great nephew of Julius Caesar. He became Caesar's heir and adopted son just before Caesar's death in 44 B.C. Octavian joined forces with Mark Antony to defeat Caesar's murderers, Cassius and Brutus, at Philippi. Octavian returned to Rome and added the title* Augustus *to his name, becoming Rome's first emperor. He died in A.D. 14.*

Gaius Julius Caesar: *He became the first Emperor of Rome. He was born in July 100 B.C., when the Roman Empire was expanding at a great pace. He was born into a noble family, and forged a distinguished career as a general and leader. Caesar was responsible for conquering Gaul and defeating various uprisings at home. His life was brought to an end at the hands of jealous Roman senators in 44 B.C.*

Vercingetorix: *Member of the Gallic Arverni tribe. A brave and intelligent warrior, he formed and led a confederation of the Gauls in a rebellion against Rome. He was defeated by and surrendered to Caesar at Alesia in 52 B.C. He was paraded in Caesar's Gallic triumph in Rome.*

School Specialty Publishing

CONTENTS

SETTING THE SCENE

In 100 B.C., at Caesar's birth, Rome was the greatest city in the ancient world. Its empire was the largest since Alexander the Great's.

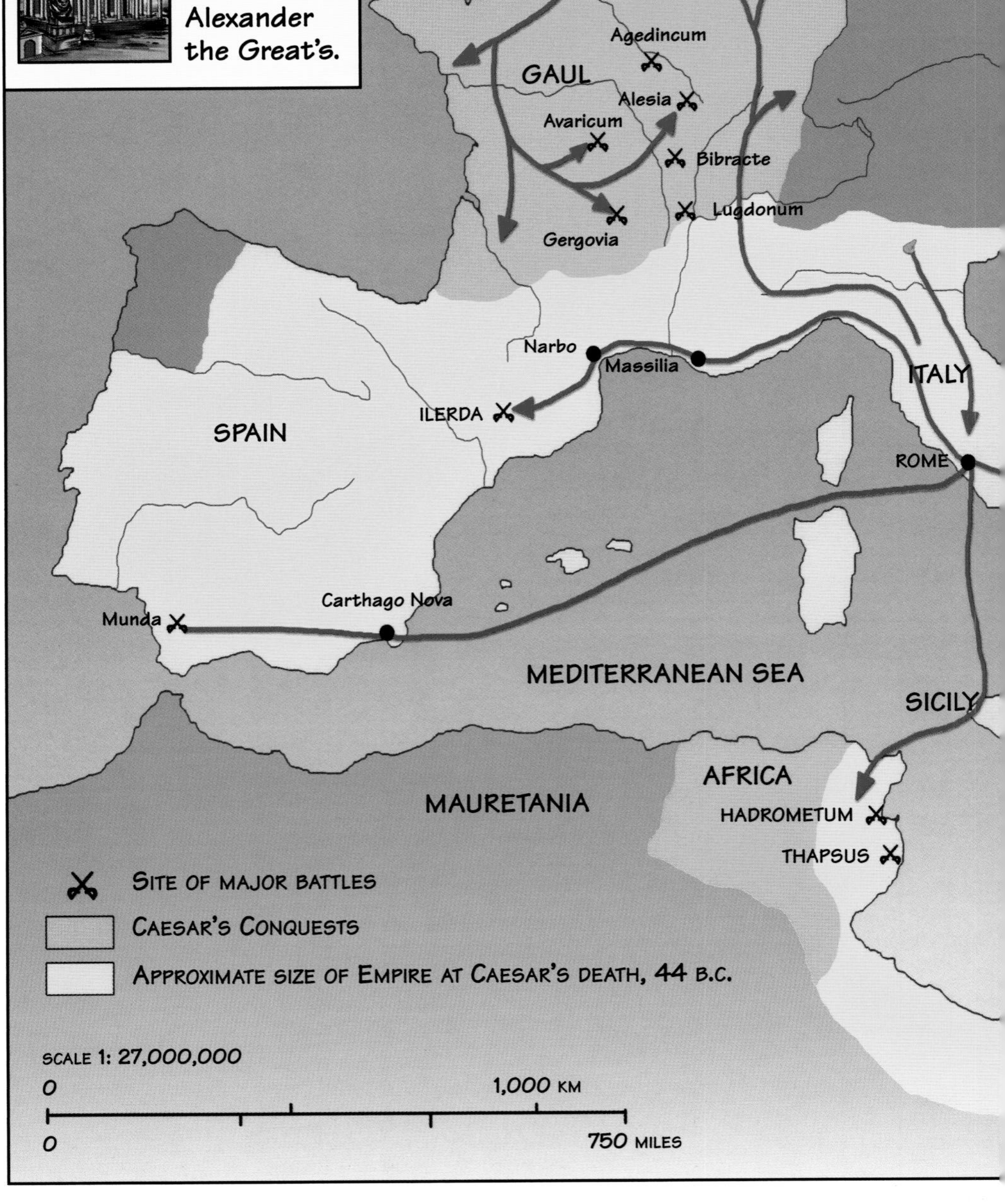

BRITANNIA

Eburone

Nervii

Agedincum

GAUL

Alesia

Avaricum

Bibracte

Lugdonum

Gergovia

Narbo

Massilia

ITALY

SPAIN

ILERDA

ROME

Carthago Nova

Munda

MEDITERRANEAN SEA

SICILY

AFRICA

HADROMETUM

MAURETANIA

THAPSUS

✗ SITE OF MAJOR BATTLES

CAESAR'S CONQUESTS

APPROXIMATE SIZE OF EMPIRE AT CAESAR'S DEATH, 44 B.C.

SCALE 1: 27,000,000

0   1,000 KM

0   750 MILES

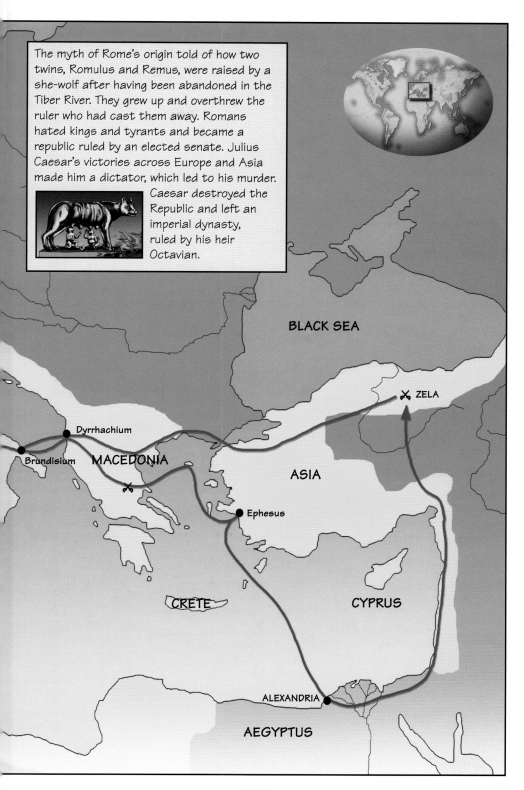

The myth of Rome's origin told of how two twins, Romulus and Remus, were raised by a she-wolf after having been abandoned in the Tiber River. They grew up and overthrew the ruler who had cast them away. Romans hated kings and tyrants and became a republic ruled by an elected senate. Julius Caesar's victories across Europe and Asia made him a dictator, which led to his murder. Caesar destroyed the Republic and left an imperial dynasty, ruled by his heir Octavian.

BLACK SEA

✗ ZELA

Dyrrhachium

Brundisium MACEDONIA

✗

ASIA

Ephesus

CRETE

CYPRUS

ALEXANDRIA

AEGYPTUS

BIRTH OF A KING

Julius Caesar's birth to an impoverished patrician family was an unremarkable event. Nevertheless, his family's status enabled him to gain important state positions at an early age. His father's death, his marriage to Cornelia, and Sulla's dictatorship of Rome were defining events in Caesar's early years.

Gaius Julius Caesar was born in July 100 B.C. in the multi-ethnic neighborhood of Rome known as Subura. His mother, Aurelia, presented their son to his father, the Roman magistrate Gaius Caesar.

Gaius, look at your handsome son. We have been blessed by the gods.

Gaius, my son and heir, you have your mother's beauty and your family's good fortune!

Caesar's mother took great care in her son's upbringing. She paid for him to be educated by one of Rome's best teachers, Marcus Antonius Gnipho, who also taught the famous speaker Cicero.

FAST FACT Caesar was Julius' family name. After his death, it was adopted by later emperors as a title. It was also adopted as a royal title in Russia (*Czar*), and in Germany (*Kaiser*).

In 88 B.C., when Julius Caesar was 12, the Roman general Sulla marched on Rome. He captured the city and strengthened the Roman Senate, taking power from the people.

Run, run! Sulla the Dictator has seized Rome!

Look! See how Rome's invincible legions flee before us!

The unrest in Rome gave the Asian king Mithridates the opportunity to wage war in Asia Minor (modern Turkey). Mithridates massacred many Romans during the uprising and caused panic in Rome.

Quick! We must escape! King Mithridates will kill us all!

In 87 B.C., when he was 13, Julius Caesar was given the lifetime honor of being appointed the High Priest of Jupiter in Rome.

Julius Caesar was given the robes of his new office during a ceremony in Jupiter's temple.

Gaius Julius Caesar, you are now the chosen one, the High Priest of Jupiter.

I will honor Jupiter and Rome. My family will be proud of me.

FAST FACT

Roman religion, a mix of old Etruscan beliefs and renamed Greek gods, was political and spiritual. Caesar's appointment as flamen dialis (High Priest) of Jupiter showed how religious offices were used to further an individual's political career.

In 85 B.C., Julius Caesar, then 15, became a man according to Roman law. In a traditional ceremony, his father gave him the *toga virilis* to wear as a sign of manhood.

Roman men dominated society, since Roman law kept women at a disadvantage. Even at a young age, patrician boys, such as Caesar, were already being groomed for a political future by being awarded important state offices.

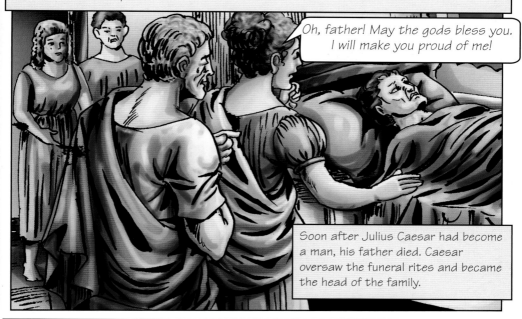

Oh, father! May the gods bless you. I will make you proud of me!

Soon after Julius Caesar had become a man, his father died. Caesar oversaw the funeral rites and became the head of the family.

At 16, Julius Caesar married for the first time. Cornelia, his wife, was the daughter of the general Lucius Cornelius Cinna. Cinna ruled Rome until Sulla recaptured it in 82 B.C.

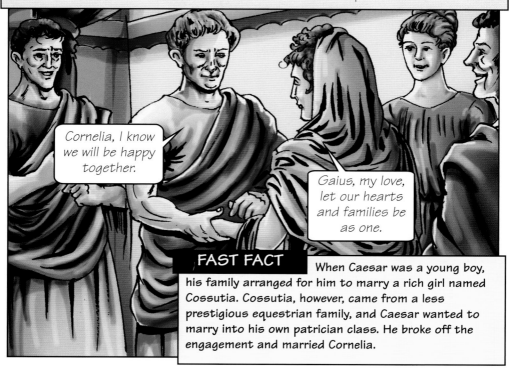

Cornelia, I know we will be happy together.

Gaius, my love, let our hearts and families be as one.

FAST FACT When Caesar was a young boy, his family arranged for him to marry a rich girl named Cossutia. Cossutia, however, came from a less prestigious equestrian family, and Caesar wanted to marry into his own patrician class. He broke off the engagement and married Cornelia.

In 81 B.C., the Dictator Sulla demanded that Caesar divorce Cornelia as a sign of his loyalty to the new regime. Caesar refused and fled Rome.

I must escape! Sulla is a sworn enemy of my wife's family!

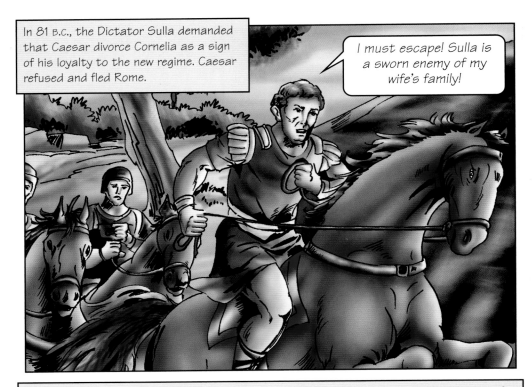

Later the same year, Sulla forgave Caesar. Caesar returned to Rome but was stripped of his office of High Priest of Jupiter. Sulla also seized Caesar's wealth, including his inheritance and Cornelia's dowry.

By order of Sulla, Dictator of Rome, Gaius Julius Caesar is no longer High Priest of Jupiter.

Julius Caesar and Cornelia had a baby daughter that same year, named Julia. She would be Caesar's only legal child.

What a beautiful daughter. The goddess Venus has smiled on us both.

May our child Julia do honor to both of our families.

Caesar's lack of a male child would change the Roman Empire in the future. Later in life, he adopted Octavian, his great-nephew, as his heir.

FAST FACT Sulla's anger at Caesar was a dangerous point in Caesar's life. Every night, Caesar stayed at a different house, bribing the owner to hide him from Sulla's secret police.

A MILITARY CAREER

In 80 B.C., the 20-year-old Caesar began his military career. He left Rome and traveled to Asia Minor. There, he served for several years under the *praetor* (provincial governor), Marcus Thermus.

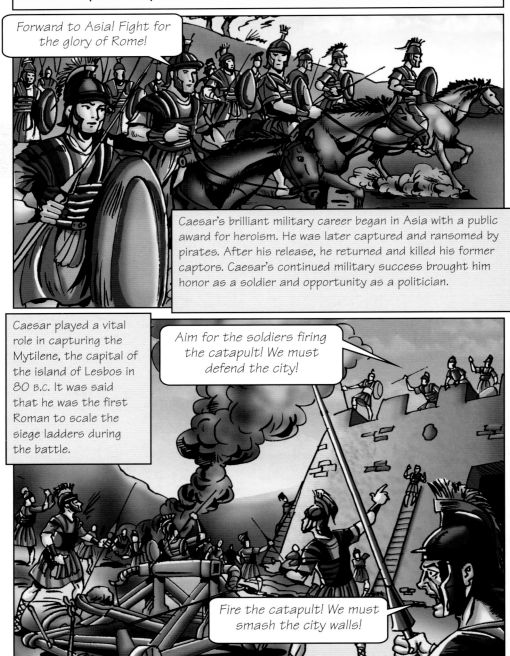

Forward to Asia! Fight for the glory of Rome!

Caesar's brilliant military career began in Asia with a public award for heroism. He was later captured and ransomed by pirates. After his release, he returned and killed his former captors. Caesar's continued military success brought him honor as a soldier and opportunity as a politician.

Caesar played a vital role in capturing the Mytilene, the capital of the island of Lesbos in 80 B.C. It was said that he was the first Roman to scale the siege ladders during the battle.

Aim for the soldiers firing the catapult! We must defend the city!

Fire the catapult! We must smash the city walls!

At Mytilene, Caesar's bravery won him the right to wear a crown of oak leaves for saving the lives of Roman soldiers in battle. He would continue to wear it throughout the rest of his life. This crown commanded respect from everyone, including senators.

Gaius Julius Casear! Take this crown of oak leaves as a sign of your bravery.

I will wear it with pride on every occasion.

When Rome heard of Caesar's victory, he was awarded a permanent seat in the Senate without any age restrictions.

Welcome, Caesar! Your heroism is rewarded with a seat in the Senate.

FAST FACT During Caesar's military service in Asia, he was said to have had an affair with Nicomedes III, king of Bithynia. Caesar's enemies never let him forget this scandal, true or not, and used it to humiliate him.

In 75 B.C., at the age of 25, Caesar sailed to Rhodes to continue his studies. He was captured on the way by pirates who sailed in the eastern Mediterranean Sea.

The pirates demanded the usual ransom of 3,000 gold pieces, but Caesar insisted that he was worth more than that. It took forty days for Caesar's followers to raise the money and gain his freedom.

Caesar had warned the pirates that, once free, he would return to capture and crucify them. Within a few months after his release, he kept his promise.

Casear kept his promise. We will all be killed now.

After defeating the pirates, Caesar sailed on to Rhodes, where he began his studies under the famous scholar, Apollonius Molon.

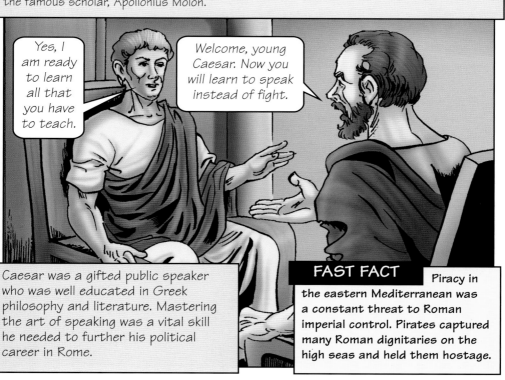

Yes, I am ready to learn all that you have to teach.

Welcome, young Caesar. Now you will learn to speak instead of fight.

Caesar was a gifted public speaker who was well educated in Greek philosophy and literature. Mastering the art of speaking was a vital skill he needed to further his political career in Rome.

FAST FACT Piracy in the eastern Mediterranean was a constant threat to Roman imperial control. Pirates captured many Roman dignitaries on the high seas and held them hostage.

At the age of 31, Caesar was appointed quaestor (finance officer) and campaigned against the tribes of Spain in 69 B.C.

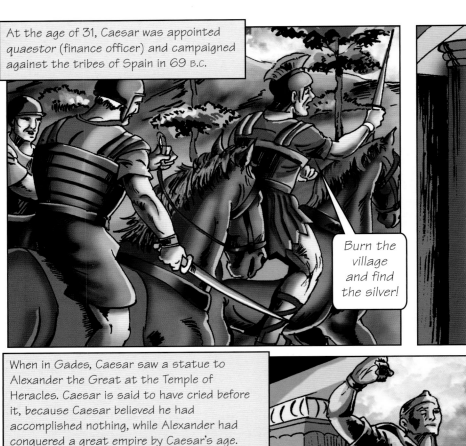

Burn the village and find the silver!

When in Gades, Caesar saw a statue to Alexander the Great at the Temple of Heracles. Caesar is said to have cried before it, because Caesar believed he had accomplished nothing, while Alexander had conquered a great empire by Caesar's age.

Great Alexander! We are the same age, but you conquered the world, and I have done nothing!

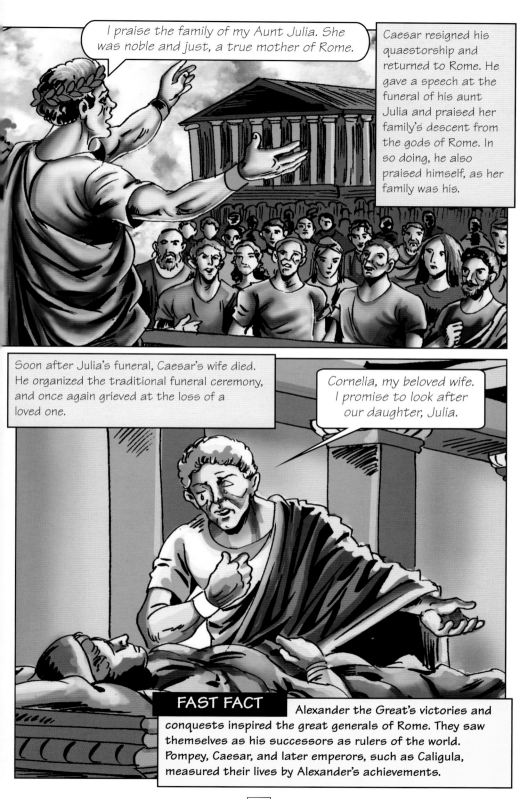

I praise the family of my Aunt Julia. She was noble and just, a true mother of Rome.

Caesar resigned his quaestorship and returned to Rome. He gave a speech at the funeral of his aunt Julia and praised her family's descent from the gods of Rome. In so doing, he also praised himself, as her family was his.

Soon after Julia's funeral, Caesar's wife died. He organized the traditional funeral ceremony, and once again grieved at the loss of a loved one.

Cornelia, my beloved wife. I promise to look after our daughter, Julia.

FAST FACT Alexander the Great's victories and conquests inspired the great generals of Rome. They saw themselves as his successors as rulers of the world. Pompey, Caesar, and later emperors, such as Caligula, measured their lives by Alexander's achievements.

Caesar married for a second time in 67 B.C. His new wife was Pompeia, the granddaughter of the Dictator Sulla and a relative of Rome's famous general, Pompey the Great.

Pompeia, let us marry and bring together the great families of Caesar and Pompey!

We must give Pompey the power to destroy the pirates that infest our seas.

In the same year, Caesar took his seat in the Senate and voted to give Pompey the authority to destroy the pirates of the eastern Mediterranean. He later gave Pompey the power to wage war on King Mithridates in Asia Minor.

In 65 B.C., Caesar became a *curule aedile* (magistrate) in Rome and controlled the city's markets, temples, and public buildings.

We must beautify Rome with new buildings.

Caesar's duties also included supervising and sponsoring Rome's public holidays and games. He organized a huge event where 320 pairs of gladiators, dressed in silver armor, fought each other and wild animals.

Aaargh!

Quick! Stab the lion in the heart!

FAST FACT Caesar knew how to appeal to Rome's population by organizing chariot races and gladiator contests. Such spectacular events were the favored entertainment of the day. Caesar's reputation soared when he spent large amounts of money on them.

POLITICAL PACTS

Caesar's re-election to High Priest of Jupiter was a crucial political achievement. Caesar now had vast wealth, looted from Spain. He became consul in 40 B.C. and forged a political group with Pompey and Crassus, the empire's wealthiest man. Together, they ruled the empire.

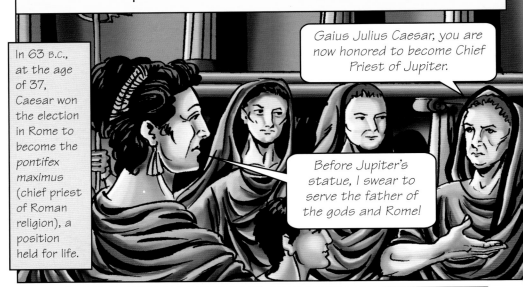

In 63 B.C., at the age of 37, Caesar won the election in Rome to become the pontifex maximus (chief priest of Roman religion), a position held for life.

Gaius Julius Caesar, you are now honored to become Chief Priest of Jupiter.

Before Jupiter's statue, I swear to serve the father of the gods and Rome!

Caesar divorced his wife, Pompeia, because she was accused of being unfaithful to him with one of Caesar's young friends, Publius Pulcher.

Go! Guilty or not, Caesar's wife must be above suspicion!

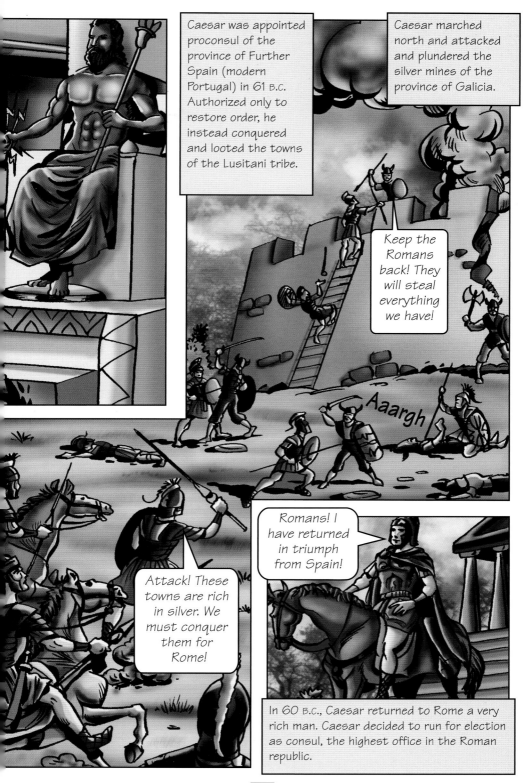

Caesar won the consulship of Rome with the help of Pompey and Marcus Licinius Crassus, Rome's richest man, in December 60 B.C.

Senators! I stand before you as consul of Rome!

Hail, Caesar! Mighty conqueror and consul!

Caesar also repaid Pompey's support and won the gratitude of the army and Rome's poor people by giving land to Pompey's veteran soldiers and the city's lower classes.

Take this land as a reward for your services to Rome!

When Caesar's political enemy, the famous Roman speaker Cato the Younger, opposed Caesar in the Senate, he was dragged from his Senate seat on Caesar's orders and thrown into jail.

Caesar, Pompey, and Crassus became the three great masters of Rome in 60 B.C. Their period of political control became known as the *First Triumvirate*.

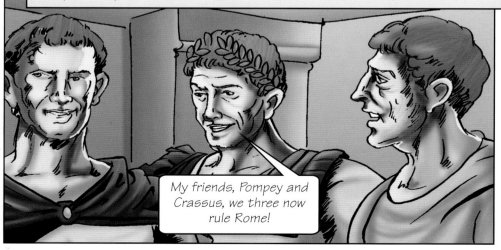

My friends, Pompey and Crassus, we three now rule Rome!

In 59 B.C., Caesar married for the third time. His new wife was Calpurnia, the daughter of Lucius Calpunius Piso, a close friend of Crassus.

Calpurnia, our marriage will bind us and safeguard the future of Rome.

Yes, Caesar! We shall be happy, and so shall everyone in Rome.

More than anything else, Caesar's marriage was a political alliance. It sealed Caesar's relationship with Crassus and rewarded Piso, who took over as consul in 58 B.C.

In the same year that Caesar married Calpurnia, Pompey married Caesar's daughter, Julia. The First Triumvirate was a group of men connected by marriage as well by as personal ambition and power.

Pompey, you shall marry my only child, my beloved daughter, Julia.

Julia, our marriage will bring us and all of Rome closer together.

One privilege of being consul was to obtain rich provinces to conquer and control after the one-year consulship finished.

Legions of Rome, we will conquer all of Gaul for the empire.

In 59 B.C., Caesar took command of Illyricum (Dalmatian Coast), Cisalpine Gaul (northern Italy), and Transalpine Gaul (southern France). A year later, he left Rome and rode north to take command of Gaul.

FAMOUS WARS

Caesar's most famous wars were against the Gauls during 58–52 B.C. His defeat of the Gallic chieftain Vercingetorix was his most important victory. He invaded Britain and Germany twice and crossed the Rubicon River to become master of Rome while Pompey fled to the Balkans. Caesar was then hailed as dictator.

We must stop the Helvetii before they invade Gaul and cause havoc.

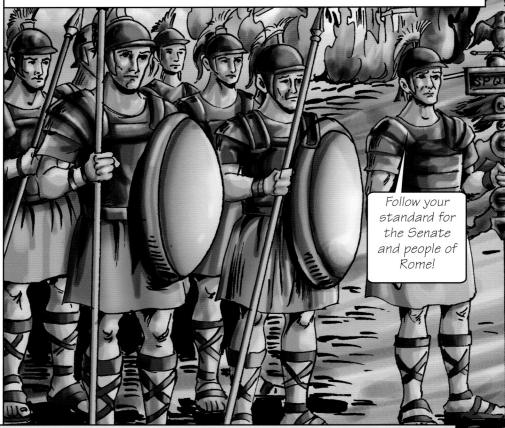

Follow your standard for the Senate and people of Rome!

Caesar's famous Gallic Wars began in 58 B.C. He marched north and attacked the Helvetii (a Swiss tribe), stopping their invasion of central Gaul. He then defeated the Germanic leader Ariovistus, who had also recently invaded Gaul.

A year later, in 57 B.C., Caesar marched his legions further north and fought against a group of Belgic tribes of northern France and Belgium. By the end of the year, all of Gaul was conquered and seemed to be at peace. Caesar defeated the rebellious Gallic tribes of the Veneti in Brittany and Normandy and the Aquitani and Cantabri in western Gaul in 56 B.C.

Charge the Gauls! If we kill their chiefs, they will flee!

In April 56 B.C., Caesar, Pompey, and Crassus met at Lucca and renewed their agreement to share power. Caesar's term as proconsul and his military command in Gaul were extended by five years.

My friends, Pompey and Crassus, we must renew our agreement!

In 55 B.C., Caesar became the first Roman to cross the Rhine river and invade Germany. He was angered by the Germanic tribes' support for the Belgic tribes in Gaul. Caesar spent 18 days ravaging German territory and intimidating the local population.

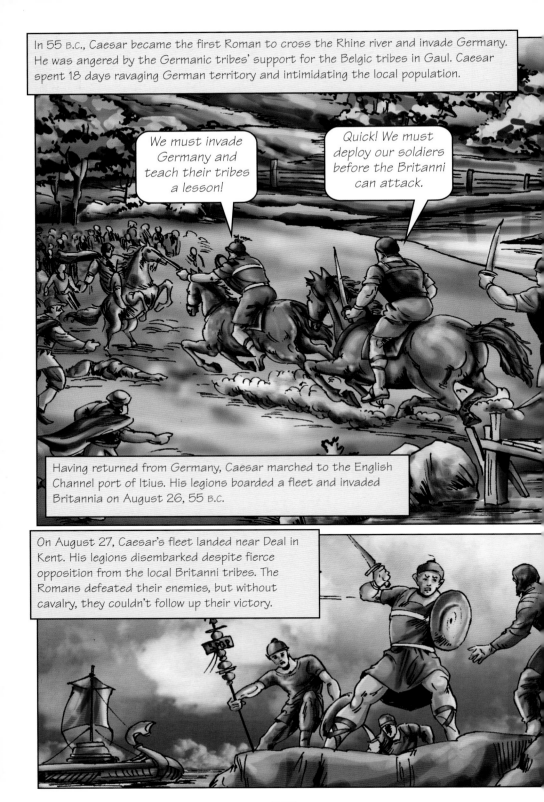

We must invade Germany and teach their tribes a lesson!

Quick! We must deploy our soldiers before the Britanni can attack.

Having returned from Germany, Caesar marched to the English Channel port of Itius. His legions boarded a fleet and invaded Britannia on August 26, 55 B.C.

On August 27, Caesar's fleet landed near Deal in Kent. His legions disembarked despite fierce opposition from the local Britanni tribes. The Romans defeated their enemies, but without cavalry, they couldn't follow up their victory.

Caesar campaigned against the Britanni tribes for several weeks. The tribes surrendered and rebelled several times. After their final surrender, Caesar returned to Gaul with his legions.

Burn their farms and destroy their villages!

What is this? They are using chariots in battle!

The Romans have few horses. We must ride them down!

Although Britannia had not been truly conquered, Caesar had reached the edge of the known world. In Rome, Pompey and Crassus organized 20 days of celebrations.

Hail, Caesar! Rome shall celebrate his victories for 20 days!

Between 55 and 52 B.C., riots and political unrest occurred in Rome while Caesar campaigned in Gaul. He returned to Britannia in 54 B.C., crossing the Thames river near London. During this time, he began losing support of the Roman Senate.

In 52 B.C., a confederation of Gallic tribes, under their leader Vercingetorix, rebelled against Roman rule. Roman towns in Gaul were burned down and their inhabitants were massacred.

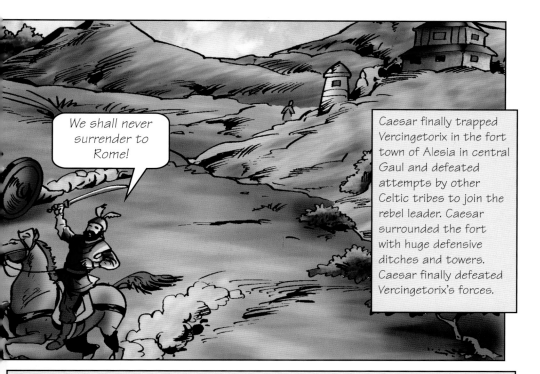

Caesar finally trapped Vercingetorix in the fort town of Alesia in central Gaul and defeated attempts by other Celtic tribes to join the rebel leader. Caesar surrounded the fort with huge defensive ditches and towers. Caesar finally defeated Vercingetorix's forces.

Vercingetorix surrendered. The day after the battle, he dressed himself in his finest armor and rode into Caesar's camp. The Gallic leader threw down his weapons and armor and knelt motionless at Caesar's feet. The rebellion was over.

By 51 B.C., Caesar was victorious in Gaul but in trouble in Rome. On January 10, 49 B.C., Caesar crossed the Rubicon River and marched his army into Italy, considered an act of war.

We must cross the Rubicon into Italy and save Rome from Pompey.

The Senate had mistakenly thought that Italian cities would reject Caesar. The Romans cheered him as he passed, instead.

Welcome, Caesar, hero of Rome!

Hurry! We must reach Rome before Pompey escapes!

Pompey fled Rome with his soldiers and senators. He marched south to Brundisium, intending to sail for the Balkans and raise new armies in the East. In the rush to escape Rome, Pompey did not take the imperial treasury.

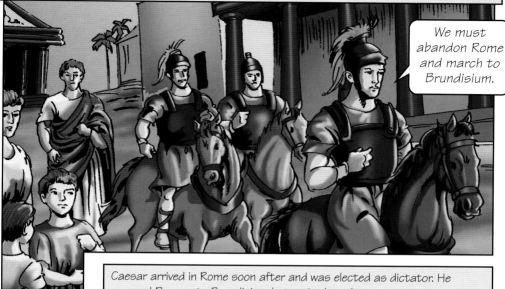

We must abandon Rome and march to Brundisium.

Caesar arrived in Rome soon after and was elected as dictator. He pursued Pompey to Brundisium but arrived too late.

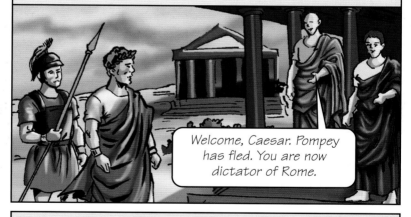

Welcome, Caesar. Pompey has fled. You are now dictator of Rome.

Pompey sailed for the Balkans on March 17, 49 B.C. However, he was unable to pay for armies or bribe the Eastern kings he had established while in power.

Sail to the East. We shall raise a new army against Caesar.

TOWARD THE END

On January 4, 48 B.C., due to a lack of transport ships, Caesar sailed for the Balkans with only half of his legions. Caesar defeated Pompey in 49 B.C., making him the most powerful man in the empire. His affair with Cleopatra made her Queen of Egypt and gave Caesar a son, Caesarion. Caesar's election as dictator for life led to his assassination in 44 B.C. Caesar's empire passed to his adopted son and heir, Octavian—who became the future emperor Augustus.

On August 9, 49 B.C., Pompey and Caesar clashed again at the town of Pharsalus. Although Pompey had more troops, he was outwitted by Caesar. Caesar marched his legions south into central Greece to find food and rest his troops. Pompey was hailed as *imperator* (emperor) and chased Caesar to fight a decisive battle.

Pompey fled the Pharsalus battlefield and sailed to Egypt. He expected a friendly welcome from the young client king, Ptolemy XIII. Instead, Pompey was murdered.

When Caesar arrived in Alexandria on October 2, Ptolemy XIII presented him with Pompey's severed head and signet ring. Caesar was angered by Ptolemy's actions.

Cleopatra, Ptolemy XIII's sister and rival for the Egyptian throne, started a long and infamous relationship with Caesar. Their relationship allowed Caesar to increase his rule even further.

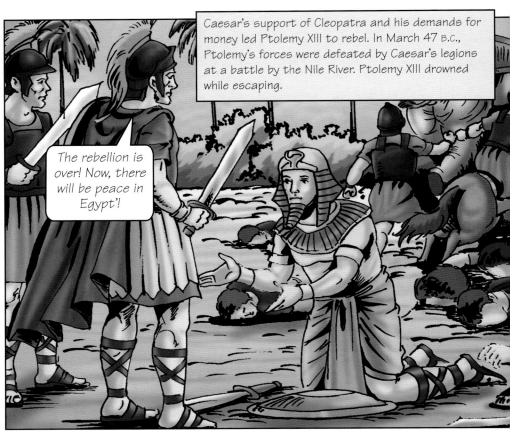

Caesar's support of Cleopatra and his demands for money led Ptolemy XIII to rebel. In March 47 B.C., Ptolemy's forces were defeated by Caesar's legions at a battle by the Nile River. Ptolemy XIII drowned while escaping.

The rebellion is over! Now, there will be peace in Egypt'!

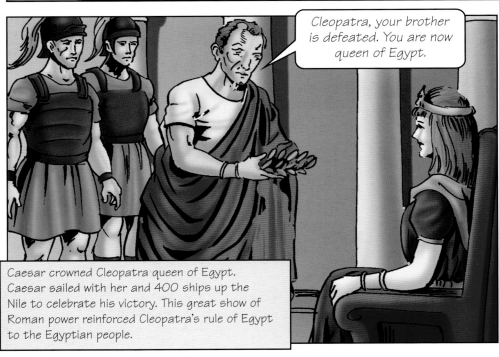

Cleopatra, your brother is defeated. You are now queen of Egypt.

Caesar crowned Cleopatra queen of Egypt. Caesar sailed with her and 400 ships up the Nile to celebrate his victory. This great show of Roman power reinforced Cleopatra's rule of Egypt to the Egyptian people.

In June 47 B.C., at 53, Caesar marched north and defeated the rebellious King Pharnaces II of Pontus (northern Turkey) at the Battle of Zela.

I came, I saw, I conquered! Asia once more belongs to Rome!

With Pharnaces defeated and Asia Minor pacified, Caesar sailed to Rome.

Caesarion, my child. One day you will be ruler of Rome and Egypt!

On June 23, 47 B.C., Cleopatra gave birth to Caesar's son in Alexandria, where she had been left under the protection of three Roman legions.

When Caesar arrived back in Rome, the Senate appointed him dictator for his victory against Pharnaces. He appointed many new senators from his army and supporters. There were several magnificent games and celebrations held in Caesar's honor.

Welcome, Caesar! We appoint you dictator for life for your services to Rome.

Great Senate of Rome, I bring victories from Greece, Egypt, and Asia.

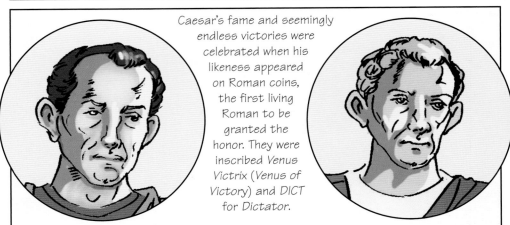

Caesar's fame and seemingly endless victories were celebrated when his likeness appeared on Roman coins, the first living Roman to be granted the honor. They were inscribed Venus Victrix (Venus of Victory) and DICT for Dictator.

Astronomers, listen! We shall reorganize the calendar. I shall have a new month named after myself, July.

Caesar was interested in administration as well as war. With the help of Cleopatra's astrologer, he reorganized the old Roman calendar to have 365 days with a leap year every 4 years. This new Julian calendar was used until 1582.

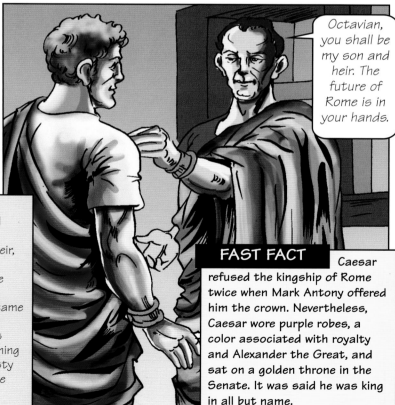

Octavian, you shall be my son and heir. The future of Rome is in your hands.

In 45 B.C., at 55, Caesar appointed his great-nephew Octavian as his heir, rather than his patrician comrade Mark Antony. Octavian also became Caesar's adopted son. Both actions marked the beginning of Caesar's dynasty and the end of the old Republic.

FAST FACT Caesar refused the kingship of Rome twice when Mark Antony offered him the crown. Nevertheless, Caesar wore purple robes, a color associated with royalty and Alexander the Great, and sat on a golden throne in the Senate. It was said he was king in all but name.

Rome's ruling class resented Caesar's increasingly authoritarian ways. They feared that he would eventually be crowned king and take away their traditional political power.

Get Caesar! Stab him now!

Even you, Brutus!? Aaagh!

Death to all tyrants!

Several days later, Caesar's funeral took place in Rome's Forum. Mark Antony gave the funeral speech before throwing a torch on the pyre. The crowd threw clothing and furniture on the fire in their grief for the greatest Roman hero.

Caesar, our hero, our god, is dead! Murdered not by Gauls, but by Romans!

To put an end to Caesar's power, he had to be killed. A well-known politician, Marcus Brutus, was persuaded to join Cassius Longinus and 60 other conspirators in the assassination.

Caesar may have suspected a conspiracy. But on the Ides of March, March 15, 44 B.C., he attended a Senate meeting in Pompey's Theatre. He was stabbed to death by the assassins.

Octavian argued with Antony and Cleopatra about who should rule Rome. Later, he defeated their armies. Antony and Cleopatra both committed suicide in Alexandria. Octavian returned to Rome, added the title Augustus to his name, and ruled as emperor until he died in A.D. 14.

After Caesar's death, Mark Antony and Octavian joined forces and defeated Cassius and Brutus in battle at Philippi in Macedonia. It is believed that Cassius committed suicide with the same dagger he used to murder Caesar.

Legions of Rome, attack and slay Caesar's murderers!

I am Caesar's son, Augustus, ruler of Rome.

TIMELINE OF CAESAR'S LIFE

Julius Caesar's life was long and violent, packed with endless battles across the ancient world and murderous political intrigues in Rome. Caesar was a brilliant general and a ruthless politician. His actions changed the shape of the Mediterranean world forever. This timeline and fast fact section provides more information on Caesar's remarkable life.

July 13, 102 or 100 B.C. (sources differ): *The birth of Gaius Julius Caesar.*

87: *Julius Caesar, 13, is named High Priest of Jupiter in Rome.*

84: *Caesar's first marriage to Cornelia, daughter of Cinna.*

81: *Caesar flees Rome to escape the hostility of the Roman dictator Sulla. Caesar and Cornelia have a daughter, Julia.*

80: *Caesar leaves Rome for military service in Asia Minor and wins the oak-leaf crown for his bravery at the siege of Mytilene on Lesbos. Caesar is permitted to sit in the Roman Senate.*

74: *Caesar fights against Mithridates' forces in Asia and returns to Rome.*

69: *Caesar's wife, Cornelia, dies.*

67: *Caesar's second marriage to Pompeia, Sulla's granddaughter.*

63: *Caesar wins election in Rome and becomes pontifex maximus.*

62: *Caesar wins the office of praetor in Rome and divorces Pompeia after a scandal.*

60: *Caesar forms the First Triumvirate with Pompey and Crassus.*

59: *Caesar marries his third wife, Calpurnia, the daughter of Piso.*

58: *Caesar begins the Gallic Wars.*

57: *Caesar and his legions fight the Belgic tribes of northern Gaul.*

56: *The triumvirate is renewed at Lucca.*

55: *Caesar's proconsulship in Gaul is extended for five years. He crosses the Rhine and then briefly invades Britain.*

54: *Caesar continues fighting in Gaul and Britain.*

53: *Caesar battles rebellious Gallic tribes.*

52: *Caesar is victorious against the Gauls. The Gallic rebellion crumbles.*

48: *Caesar defeats Pompey at the Battle of Pharsalus on August 9. Caesar arrives in Alexandria and meets Cleopatra.*

47: *Caesar is elected dictator again. He defeats the Egyptian army under Ptolemy XIII and destroys the rebellion of Pharnaces II at Zela in Asia Minor. Cleopatra gives birth to Caesar's son, Caesarion.*

46: *Caesar is elected consul for third time. He defeats Pompeian forces at the Battle of Thapsus and is elected dictator for 10 years.*

45: *The Roman Senate elects Caesar dictator for life. Caesar's image appears on coins. Octavian becomes his heir and adopted son.*

44: *Caesar refuses to be crowned king. He is murdered by Cassius, Brutus, and 60 other conspirators on March 15 at a Senate meeting.*

42: *Caesar is deified. Cassius and Brutus commit suicide after being defeated by Octavian and Mark Antony at Philippi.*

DID YOU KNOW?

1. *During Caesar's lifetime, the Roman Empire extended from Gaul (France) in the north, south to Spain, and east to Asia (Turkey), Egypt, and Palestine. It was the largest empire since Alexander the Great's (356–323 B.C.).*

2. *The Roman army excelled in military discipline and tactics. Roman siege engines and towers destroyed enemy fortresses. The testudo formation allowed legionaries to link their shields together and advance under the shield's protection.*

3. *The Roman empire was built on slavery. 150,000 captives were sold as slaves after just one battle in Macedonia in 168 B.C. Slaves could be killed or freed by their masters. By A.D. 400, eight of ten Roman families had slave ancestry.*

4. *Caesar was a gifted writer, speaker, and general. He wrote fascinating and detailed memoirs of his military campaigns. These stories also helped him achieve his political goals. His account of the Gallic Wars was his most famous writing.*

5. *Caesar's victories in Gaul were his greatest military achievement. He stormed 800 cities, vanquished 300 tribes and killed one million Gauls. He also took another million Gauls prisoner and sold an additional million into slavery.*

6. *While campaigning in Britannia, Caesar saw that very few inhabitants planted corn. Most lived on milk and meat. These people wore animal skins and painted themselves blue to give them a fierce look.*

7. *The predictable annual flooding of the Nile made Egypt a very rich agricultural land. Fleets of grain ships sailed from Alexandria to Rome to sell their harvest.*

8. *To make himself popular in Rome, Caesar began many new buildings in 46 B.C. These included a new Senate house, a great marketplace called the* Basilica Julia, *a new state library, and a temple to his ancestor, the goddess Venus.*

9. *Pompey's wife, Caesar's daughter Julia, died in 54 B.C. Crassus died in battle in 53 B.C. With the Triumvirate broken, Pompey was swayed by Caesar's enemies in the Senate, setting the stage for Caesar's march on Rome.*

10. *At the Battle of Thapsus in 46 B.C., near Carthage in North Africa, Caesar destroyed the last of Pompey's remaining forces. The speaker Cato committed suicide after this.*

11. *Caesar was elected dictator four times. He became dictator for life in 44 B.C., just before his death. He was assassinated during a meeting of the Senate. At the time, the Senate building itself was being rebuilt with Caesar's own money. In 42 B.C., Caesar was deified (named as a god).*

12. *Augustus used his imperial power to finish many of Caesar's plans, which turned the Roman Republic into a Mediterranean empire of 60 million people. Augustus established the* Pax Romana *(Roman Peace).*

GLOSSARY

Aedile: *Roman official whose rank was below that of praetor but above quaestor.*

Alexandria: *Egyptian port capital founded by Ptolemy, one of Alexander the Great's generals. It rivaled Rome's size and magnificence. It was where the ruling dynasty lived. That dynasty ended with Cleopatra's suicide.*

Amphitheaters: *Public buildings that served as arenas for celebrations as well as contests between gladiators.*

Asia: *Roman province that covered the area of modern western Turkey.*

Centurion: *Roman army staff officers in charge of between 100 and 1,000 soldiers. There were normally about 60 centurions in a legion.*

Circus Maximus: *Rome's largest racetrack where 150,000 spectators could watch and bet on chariot races.*

Cisalpine Gaul: *Roman province covering the area that is modern-day northern Italy.*

Client king: *Rulers of kingdoms beyond the boundaries of the Roman empire who were given their rule by Rome. They were controlled by Rome's rulers.*

Cohort: *Roman army unit. There were 10 cohorts to a legion, each divided into 6 centuries.*

Consul: *The supreme elected civil and military office in Rome. Each consulship lasted for one year, though consuls could be re-elected and serve several terms.*

Dictator: *The supreme and originally temporary Roman office held by an individual in times of emergency. Sulla became dictator but then resigned, and Caesar held the office three times before becoming dictator for life. The post no longer existed after his death.*

Forum: *The main public square of a town or city where temples and the main civic buildings were located.*

Further Spain: *A Roman province in south-central Spain. The main cities were Corduba and Gades. It was neighbored by Nearer Spain and Lusitania (Portugal).*

Gaul: *Roman province of what is modern-day France and Belgium.*

Gladiators: *Usually criminals and prisoners of war, gladiators were highly trained professional killers who fought each other and wild animals for public entertainment in amphitheatres across the Roman empire.*

Illyricum: *Roman province covering the area between Bosnia and Albania.*

Imperator: *Title used by Roman emperors to indicate status. More generally used to salute Roman military commanders after a victory.*

Insulae: *The multi-story apartment blocks where most Romans lived. The term means* island. *Crowded and dirty, insulae had no running water or sewers.*

Jupiter: *Father of the gods in the Roman religion. In many ways, he was simply the Roman equivalent of the Greek god Zeus. He was the protector of Rome and its people.*

Legion: *The main unit of the Roman army. Each legion had 5,000 infantry, 120 cavalry, and additional auxiliary troops.*

Patrician: *The group of aristocratic Roman families who traced their origins to Rome's earliest days. There were 14 patrician clans, each with 30 families.*

Plebeian: *The group of non-patrician Roman citizens.*

Praetorian guard: *Imperial bodyguards created by Augustus. It originally only had 1,000 soldiers.*

Pontifex Maximus: *The most prestigious elected religious office in Rome, literally* the highest of all priests. *This office was held for life.*

Praetor: *Second in authority only to the consul. Praetors were state officials. Originally, there were 12 praetors. The most important was the praetor urbanus (city praetor).*

Quaestor: *Lowest office of state that a senator could hold. Quaestors often served as finance officers, reporting to a provincial governor.*

Senate: *The supreme council of the Roman state whose senators were recruited from quaestors. Augustus fixed its membership at 600. Each senator needed to own property worth 10,000 gold pieces (1 million sesterii).*

Transalpine Gaul: *Roman province covering the area that is modern-day southern France.*

Tribune: *An office that formed part of a plebeian senator's career. Originally, as tribunes of the people, the office holder was expected to protect Roman citizens by using their vote to pass laws.*

Triumph: *The grand procession through Rome awarded to a victorious Roman general. The triumph ended at the Temple of Jupiter. After Augustus, only emperors had triumphs.*

Vestal Virgins: *Six women that served the goddess Vesta in her temple next to Rome's Forum. They served for 30 years.*

INDEX